LIGHT BLOOMS

MICHAEL THOMAS KELLY

MOTHER'S HEN Berkeley

1993

Mother's Hen

P.O. Box 695
Berkeley, CA 94701-0695

Library of Congress Catalog Card No.: 93-77575
ISBN: 0-914370-59-6

Typesetting & Technical Assistance by Regent Press
Photos by Marty Kaliski
Edited by Robert Lavett Smitt
Co-published with:

Coiled Hands Imprint
c/o Michael Thomas Kelly
P.O. Box 3376
San Leandro, CA 94578-0376

This book of poems is dedicated to the
matriarch which lies within me;
Cecilia Cuff Olofson, Madelyn Allen Kelly,
Patricia Kelly Oliver, Mariah Young,
Mother, mommy, and Michael.

A special thanks to Steve Arnstsen
for his honesty and artistic integrity.
Yes, of course, he too, is worthy and deserving of our love.

ACKNOWLEDGMENTS

The people who do my forewords, the introductions to my books are more famous and in many ways are more dedicated, devoted and delightful, brightly shining lights in the poetry skies.

Again, I thank them for their contributions.

Presses, Printers, Typesetters, Calligraphers, Artists, Photographers, Graphixists, and the list goes on toward infinite details and certain insanity if it were not for editors, publishers, aide-de-camps, supporters and fans.

But most of all this book was done with the sadness of the absence of Dick Ellington, though I constantly felt his watchful eyes appropriately guiding.

Other dead people of note are my older brother, my father, my older sister and all of my grandparents.

Amongst the living are those people who defy categories or are in multiple categories like: friend, colleague, impresario, technician, relative, confidante, lover.

TABLE OF CONTENTS

TABLE OF CONTENTS *(con't)*

LIGHT BLOOMS

PREVIOUS IMPRINTS

NIGHTS INTO WHITE STARS

I tell you the past is a bucket of ashes.
– Carl Sandburg, *Cornhuskers,* 1918

I remember well the Spring of 1960.
John F. Kennedy campaigned in Illinois.
Sitting on the back seat of a convertible waving;
the limo drove from the Moline, Illinois
airport down 17th Street across
the Centennial Bridge (yes, the Mississippi River)
to the Davenport, Iowa airport.
I lived on 16th Street; the parade route
was only a block away
and I rode
my bike alongside the Democratic Candidate
for president of the United States.
At a slow down to stop, I shook his hand.
And I believed in a just God and
order came from chaos.
The first Catholic president would be a Democratic
Party Candidate and the Irish were cleansed.
Wealth and power came to those who smiled;
were young and lovely.
And I believed that if all of us tried hard
even Negroes could be freed. After all, God was good and
those who were good deserved to live good.

It was early in my senior year
of high school when the classroom security,
safety, and serenity was shattered by the brown box
on the wall playing the radio report
that John F. Kennedy was shot dead by assassins' bullets
while sitting in the back seat of a convertible waving as
the limo drove from the airport on a parade route.

I was dressed in my good clothes watching T.V.;
waiting for Dad to start the car;
waiting for the parade route to Sunday Mass down 15th Street.
I saw Jack Ruby shoot Lee Harvey Oswald
while in the custody of cops in Dallas before cameras; live.
(Jack Ruby died not convicted.)
The drum roll cadence; staccato live on cameras;
on T.V. the flag draped coffin in a horse
drawn cart and a riderless horse on T.V.
cameras all along the parade route.
Through it all, I still believed God was good
and with good schooling comes success and
that a majority of past presidents of the United States
were lawyers. After I completed law school
even I could be a president of the United States.

It was another three years or so in the November
nite of a Chicago "el" train ride that I looked
at the soot on my hands and face from the foundry.
The Black, Dark Soot of Smoke and Dust
clogged and freckled my skin.
White eyes stared like some minstrel show caricature
at the Black, Dark, Squalid landscape that clogged
the streets and skies. As the "el" train rumbled,
I doubted that there was a God let alone whether he, she, or it was
good. I wished the "el" train would
silently plunge from the elevated, stilted tracks
and forever plunge into the deepest abyss of Negative,
Neither, and Nihilism. Chicago was like falling in love with a
prostitute and Richard J. Daley
was the head pimp. I saw him lead the
parade down State Street on St. Patrick's Day
and the Irish were clean; the Democratic
Party was blessed; Catholics were good; and urbane loveliness
prevailed.

I had to leave Chicago.
I couldn't go east into deeper,
darker, urban filth.
I was infected with the venereal disease
of urban squalor. I returned home
for the cure in Rock Island, Illinois.
Then after a long recuperative period, periodically
shattered by the assassinations of Malcolm X, Rob't Kennedy,
Martin Luther King, Jr., Kent St. students, Jackson St. students,
and on and on; I took what was left of my sanity
down to 17th Street and crossed the Mississippi
River one more time on the Centennial Bridge
out past the Davenport airport to Interstate 80
and hitchhiked to Arizona arriving
in the West on the Ides of March, never
stopping to ask if God was good;
if God was or
if God or
if.

ZERO GRAVITY

(Adagio)

Every pilot I've ever met likes to take passengers
to zero gravity. It's easy and unassuming.
Climb to ten-twenty thousand feet (or meters
if you're scientific) –
Then at nite over The City with a quick flip of the stick it's

(con muy muchismo gusto – prestissimo con brio)

Headlights, street lights, car lights, stop lights, go lights
Lite beer, light headed, Neon light, Bay's lighthouse –
Bridge's lights, boat lights, harbors' lites, birds alight, dockside,
interior lights, exteriors, bright beams, low beams,
whirling emergency red lights, white lights, blue,
BART train beams, circles of lights, sky lights, skyscrapers'
lights – City lights . . . Nose up
Moonlight and starslights against the Night *(Andante)*
Beaming pilot's white teeth saying
"Now wasn't that fun?"

COMPACT DISC

The other day I was reading about superconductivity
when I fell asleep and began visualizing my
dream. I stood in front of the window as the sun
shone through the pristine glass and the sky
was a blue between azure and cobalt. And sun's
warmth glistened as the first tear fell and I realized it was true –
The tear refracted sunlight and fractured rainbows
into pure colors while I faced knowing it was so.
The Reagan Administration has now spent our
National Endowment
and we are beyond broke – The debt is greater than all other
Presidents' combined – Ronald Reagan and Richard Nixon
bought guns and destroyed our space program and I
shall never travel in space as promised by John F. Kennedy.
The tears fell and now we know we shall never see space
only tearful disgust for shadowy profligates who've
squandered our fortunes.
And opening a dowry found a multi-trillion-
dollar I.O.U.
And I saw my life unravel before me like some
unfolding of paper dolls and cut-out doilies.
My life uncoiled like strands of concertina
wire atop a security fence –
Then
And I was asleep and I awakened
And I was dark everywhere around me
As I woke up I realized I'd awakened
into the sublime – You'd left the music on
playing Tschaikovsky and climbed into bed
and we were next to each other. Now
I was awake and you were asleep and the symphony
played and a skyful of stars shone and I knew
that our intimacy burnished, rubbed smooth
the harshness of reality that only
a skyful of stars can redeem.

immense concentration

great blue heron on stilts stalks thru silt and marsh
of former oyster bed hunting silvery white and grey
wrigglers of shallow waters;
then halts – freeze frame – standing motionless – eyes silent waits;
while lowest water in six months ebbs near marina area;
while winged gulls glide and soar with the winds
that winterly bluster over mello drama
of feeding fowls; killdeers at waterline pecking,
aquatic ducks floating on choppy waters;
while jetliners cargoed with people land into airport crosswinds;
while din of not so distant interstate highway rumbles and
lovers and cars and pick-ups cruise and cops
patrol and peopled fishing poles, joggers, frolickers
and picnickers parade along the shoreline; while garish
sails and boats ànd catamarans are sailing;
while birdwatchers watch
and others feed birds into semi-tameness
ZHAATTT
the great blue heron feeds today.

YELLOW WINDOWS

> "I've seen it all, I've seen it all
> thru the yellow windows of the
> evening train . . ."
> – Tom Waits, Rain Dogs;
> 9th & Hennepin, 1985

& the clickety clacks of those railroad tracks
rocks me to sleepy naps of no dreams
and narcotized drunken sadness
& the train trip two thousand miles old rattles
onward into yesterday's nitemares, prattles
senseless beauty of broad openness
of another thousand miles of mountains
and deserts & the clickety clacks of those
railroad tracks racing through another city's
backyards and factories' back doors –
Then I stare thru Tom Waits' yellowed windows
into the dark eyes of deep awe and innocence
of children beside their bicycles & plotting their escape
to the melody of the clickety clacks of those
railroad tracks – It's
them, the children with their eyes that stare
at me and those railroad tracks plotting my escape
to the rhythm of the pounding of the clickety clacks
of those railroad tracks
    I stare at the children; they stare at me;
we hear the clickety clacks of those railroad wheels
    I am the children thirty, forty, years ago
staring at the men in the yellowed windows
of the passing train who stare at me, the child
as the railroad wheels pound out the rhythm
of the clickety clacks of those railroad tracks
& the deep, dark eyes of the children are the same
in every different city; different children in every
same city at the railroad crossings
the constant clickety clacks of those railroad tracks.

Out of the corners of your eyes   you watch

your peripheral vision is working   rapidly

as you attempt to sit   casually   at this bus stop

your bus stop   the one you go to when you are

going home after shopping   eating   drinking

orange   blue hair and black   silver leather

needs your watching   she is animated

and speaks   somewhat loudly with her chilly voice

on this grey cloudy day   about to rain

as bursts of wind gather leaves and papers

and then rearrange them

she is smoking cigarettes and wishing she had more money

then as quick as she appeared   she explodes

exploding into a puff of gray green and purple smoke
but the cloud stops expanding and collapses
into a piece of plastic whatever trash
and swirls with the leaves and papers
redefining beauty in another galaxy   universe   existence

and now you know why you are

always afraid when you see them

brash   trash   punk   funk with spunk

their colors always colliding

their molecules too unstable

sometime   on this planet   at this bus stop

you too may explode

your colors will critically collide

and your molecules collapse

you must watch out for them

they may contaminate you with animation

life   a life worth dying

kristallnacht

i was the brain matter who spattered
and splattered your face & glasses joseph himmler
when your ss goon shot me point black in front of you
you even had the human decency to recoil and quaver
I gave you my answer to the situation
more jews more jews than you can transport
more jews than you can process more jews
than you can kill more jews than you can
bury or hide
your reply was known eventually the whole world knew
more efficient killing but my answer
outlived yours there will always be jews
the truth awaits your embrace
shattering your stereotypical realities
like a pane of storefront glass in a ghetto
on the night of crystal

for all those people who had
blue numerical tattoos on their forearms

THE SILVER OF LAS BALLEÑAS

I. The Overture

Precaucion: este camino
no esta para alta velocidad.
South of La Jolla and into Tejota
the road signs issue the warning.
Caution: this road is not
for high speed.
For years I have listened at camp's fireside
to the stories and tales of great
wealth of the Silver from Las Balleñas.
It's not known if the silver comes from caves,
diggings or mines.
Con cuidado ustedes quines hablan español.
Es posible que ustedes no saben
que son las balleñas.
Beware you who speak in Spanish; it is possible
you don't know Las Balleñas.
It may not be where (or even who)
you may think it is.
The tellers of tales come from everywhere
The Californians with their superlatives
The Texans with their grandiosities
The Alaskans with their verities
Some say seven cities;
others say gold. But liquor, the poor man's
truth serum, speaks of silver. I, the former
barkeep, now know, from reading books and from
the distillates' speeches; I have distilled the necessary
knowledge of the Silver of Las Balleñas.

Many times I pushed away and resisted the drinks
of ethanol and pocketed the monies, tips
and pieces of gold and silver.

Now here on the – sin drogas – I am drug-free . . .
South of Ensenada ten-twenty years ago,
the road ended; then in the early seventies
the transpeninsular road was built – And now,
where the old road ended, the new road begins.
And now I, two score and more, am well-traveled
on the mainland roads. I speak the language
but more important, I dig the diggers' lingo.
I push onward, "Damn Ahab"
towards the middle of the spine of mountains.
Onward towards the land beneath the mountains
where the desert drops to its knees
to meet the sea; turkey vultures
sweep the sky.

II. The Fugue

It has become necessary to have guides, assistants
and sherpas. After several days in Guerro Negro, we
head west to the whalers' lagoon. Stories retold
and reheard are that of the first whaler who
spotted the first whales – killed the calves to attract
the mothers and others – the babies' screams then killed all.
But they kept coming, the whales and the whalers, till
the killing killed itself in order to preserve itself,
its Self, its selflessness. The pain of childbirth
outweighs the fear of danger; it's not a matter of courage
do not ask the mother to choose; there is no choice.
We secure a boat and we'll sail to Bahia Tortugas
in Scamon's lagoon as dawn is upon Laguna Ojo de Liebre.
At nite when the wind is right,
I hear the drone of machines turning;
of diesels churning.

Is there mining near Bahia Tortugas?
Turtles Bay on the map is blurred and parched . . .
The local nacionales differ in their directions.
The kayak is readied for dawn departure.

Nite Time
then First Light

The oars glisten in the unrisen sun's first light.
Light that's golden against azul of sky
brown of land and green to purple of sea
and white of fog and haze, "Damn Ahab!"
"Damn Ahab," the rowing's hard – the muscles ache,
wanting to separate from bone and skin wants to burn
from the flesh from the sun. The pain's getting greater,
the tides pulling one way; the winds another;
our direction in still another. The aches I've known
to get here are greater than that of the multigravida
but no stopping; I'm almost there.

Then the back of whale appears. It is black, grey
and shines. It is grey and the barnacles appear.
It is silver and the tail splashes the water
sending spray into the air.
And again the spouting of air from the blow hole;
air from the lungs condenses in the morning sunlight,
silver. I have in my face the silver of las balleñas.

Blow Baby, Mother Fluke

The turbulence overturns the boat and I
am sinking. There is falling away . . .
I feel the existential leap into the Quantumized . . .
Ahab, the staunch one with mutilated reality,
limb, and sex organs.
He wears the face of my father
And my father's father

and my mother's grandfather
and he is god-like, also named Michael
with a flaming sword and an Archangel, too.
Black-brimmed with Super-Ego Sombrero.

He must go . . .
        Zarathustra speaks saying,
"Now you can eat feeding on more than just krill,
shrimp, and shellfish.
You can dive deep and hunt predators;
Down deep till you can feed
on your own illusions . . .
You know both sides
of the contradiction; seeing
how they fit and why they work . . ."

        Down deeper I plunge
thru Dante's rings: four, five, seven, nine
and punch thru
And with Jim Morrison's microphone and guitar
break thru the other side; it is a black hole
Janis, Jimi, Otis –
Bix and pork-pie hatted horn blower –
I see the Scribner,
hear the Scribner saying,
"I'd rather not . . ." and
Melville's desperation
Damn Ahab
Ahead the precipice,
the abyss, awaits.

Now knowing who Ahab is –
Ahab, the polarizing foundamentalist
frozen, polymerized, spinning
in his own orbit; unable to leap

to the next level – He must die; Ahab must die.
The Jihad is over –
The Crusader is too far from home;
too close to the Grail.
Damn Ahab
Rule Number One: the pain and suffering
causes confusion and delusion.

There, the Bodhisattva emanates from within Las Balleñas
sharing the same saffron light from within me –
within me suffused in silver light threads are
a million whales; a million bodhisattvas;
miliones de Las Balleñas.

I see the tree that is with me
seeing across six thousand years
of branches that bloom two hundred,
three hundred blossoms of life times
that were me; some fruits have fallen
on the ground.

The greatest good for the greatest number
Above all, serve all and be happy
Take impish delight in afflicting the comforted
Take compassion in comforting the afflicted.

Take compassion in comforting the afflicted
Take impish delight in afflicting the comforted
But above all serve all and be happy.

I am dry. I was never wet.
I am cleansed. I was never dirty.
This is Tien there never was a Sheol
This is Nirvana there always was illusion
Now there is illumination.

III. The Cadenza

The drunken boat returns
to shore tired and exhausted.

I hear the drone of diesels from Bahia Tortugas,
a cannery for the catch from the fish camps.
The drunken boat returns to the shore
tired and drained.
There is rumination of redemption
and salvation.

Yes, it is clearer thru rumination;
to samsara – enlightenment
then to Nirvana.
The Hawk from the mountain's cliff
flies to the sea; dives into the flock
of aquatic birds huddling, scurrying
together guarding their clutches.

Back on the road home,
we stop for gas
the tip-man washes
our car windows.
He asks with toothless smiles
for propina.
We give him the silver of Las Balleñas.

Save the Whales!
The whales save us.
If they die we are already dead.

WOMEN

At the window while watching
washing dishes or clothes
As my mother did
as her mother did
At the window watching, the sunlight
into the sink through the curtains
watching the sink
Dreaming of another lover
or the other that wasn't
and how it could've been
Thinking of what's best
for her children
At the window at the sink
watching the sunlight
watching across the lawn,
across the street, across the river,
lake, bay or ocean; watching at the doorstep
watching . . .

EARLY IMPRINTS

THE ASHEN PEACOCK

That nite we danced, dined, and wined.
The Phoenix and I flittered till our wings hurt,
That blissful nite we let our hearts unwind.
But through our hair came the Seventh Wind.

You're ashed. Soon to fly to a higher tier.
Rebirth shall give our hearts a tighter bind.
For there's trickling from my eye – a tear.
Love's false hope, tugging starts to tear.

And I remember days spent and nite's dessert.
Then that wind came, upsetting curls, tearing hair,
Gnashing teeth; useless screams are heard in the desert,
Knowing false hope, love too, shall soon desert.
And my forehead's filled with sweat, my mind – fear,
Leaving me only memory's black smear.

1968-9

Twenty-five
Haikus

by Mikelly
1970

These haikus are for and caused by all the people I love.

I picked a daisy
and plucked the petals,
hoping it lied:

"She loves me not . . . "

Mikelly
Iowa
ix-1970

Haiku One

I. Rain falls on aspen
As newly formed streams flow
to one huge ocean.

iv-27-70
Albuquerque

Lenora's Haiku

II. Sand grains causing pain;
There's a dust storm in town today.
Head winds make walk slow.

v-1-70

Haiku for Young Gloria

III. The wind pushes a cloud.
Below my love comes to me
like cold air to warm.

vii-17-70

Kool-Aid Haiku

IV. The stream, swift and cool
aids me in my wanderings;
softens me within.
(For Wm. J. somewhere high in the Andes)

vii-20-70

Haiku V

V. Lightning flashes
across a black summer sky,
Forewarns sudden rain.

vii-23-70

<u>Haiku VI</u>

VI. Rainbow arches clouds
touching pined mountain peaks.
The rain has passed.

vii-23-70

<u>Haiku VII</u>

VII. Still water reflects
a dim moon behind the clouds;
Rain begins to fall.

viii-17-70

<u>Texas Haiku</u>

VIII. Thru the midnite air
a full moon dances with stars;
the rain clouds are spent.

viii-19-70
Dallas

<u>Return Haiku</u>

IV. Can't wait to return,
Eleven days since departure.
The sun's sure to shine!

ix-10-70
Nebraska

<u>Iowa Haiku</u>

V. Alfalfa bundles
await winter's storage barn
Before the frost comes.

ix-70
Iowa

Haiku Eleven

XI. Grasshoppers jumping
in fallow fields of clover;
Next year's corn supply.

ix-70
Iowa

Haiku Twelve

XII. Pheasants in a field
wing with their mates
knowing the
Dread of the huntsmen.

ix-70
Iowa

Haiku Thirteen

XIII. The trees shed their leaves
as black bears curl into warm
fetal positions.

ix-11-70
Albuquerque

Haiku Fourteen

XIV. A squirrel scampers
in leaf strewn lawns
searching for
a winter hide-out.

ix-11-70

Lover's Haiku

XV. The soft summer breeze
caresses the breast of my love,
protecting her dreams.

ix-11-70

Sunset Haiku

XVI. The day's sun deflates
into a Western mesa
echoing nightfall.

ix-12-70

Functionalism Haiku

XVII. Fountain's water
supply performs no function;
but beautiful falls.

ix-12-70

Haiku Eighteen

XVIII. The sun murmurs death,
fading below Western skies;
Nightfall's released.

ix-18-70

Sunrise Haiku

XIX. The eastern sunlight
chases the darkness from the sky;
Another day awaits.

ix-16-70

Lightning Haiku

XX. The nite's sky is black,
no stars before the storm starts;
Lightning slashes – START.

ix-16-70

<u>Love Haiku</u>

XXI. Love grows with only
infinity to bound it;
washing away walls.

ix-18-70

<u>Vedic Haiku (for Dr. Charlene)</u>

XXII. Moksa is beyond;
but today's horizon hides
a one-legged cow.

ix-20-70

<u>Upanisads-I Haiku</u>

XXIII. A love affair with
nature's gossamer womb;
TRANSCENDENTALISM.

ix-23-70

<u>Upanisads-II Haiku</u>

XXIV. A light streaks across
seen and then evaporates
in misty auras.

ix-23-70

<u>Upanisads-III Haiku</u>

XXV. Om A-U-M Om
(seven silent syllables)
Be Adoration.

ix-23-70
Albuquerque

"It's a grave yard we look
across tonite." Abraham Lincoln

Auto[mation?] Grave Yard

Clink
Clank
Clunk

Here we pile the junk
The men I've been in bed with are many
~~In bed Ive been with~~ 1102-48
But from none Ive taken a penny
Whose debts these are
I dont know
From your body
Life blood will flow
through the
Willows the breeze will blow *T.S. Thanks
Whose winds these are you
Think you know
Here we pile the junk

Clink
Clank
Clunk

* * * *

What Is Poetry

I. Poetry is a thought put to beauty
Define thought and beauty
And you have poetry

II. A thought in beauty
And what is beautiful?
To this I say, "to each his own"
And this is the poem

What Poetry Is

SHADOW

Then a passing lite in the
nite shines.

She knows not what
She knows what not
but intuitively,
but intuitively smiles.
Knowing the way
she does, it will fade
flicker and fade.

Justifiably she was
looking for a sight
to break the silence

Some one once told
her that lites are
happy and only

darkness is lonely.

* * * *

YOU CAN WIPE THE SMILE FROM YOUR FACE

You can wipe the kiss from your lips
And I can wipe the blood from my wound
I can peel the crustation from my wound
No nerve endings to regenerate

Scars are insensitive to a second laceration
It only hurts to destroy sensitivity
From subsequent lacerations.
Can come quick recuperation.

BROWN & GREEN, #12 – PART II

The autumn embers burn low
The faucet freezes
A brass poker stirs the midnite ashes
As wolves howl in swirling winds
Of a snowstorm that blows
Across a once rippling stream
Now silenced by its frozen
Sheet and wintertime lid
        But Then
I saw a songbird, pregnant,
Full of Life in the budding
Branches of a willow tree
Warmed by the spring breeze
And sunlight which caught
My dimming sight and renewed
The fast fading me and gave
To me a hope in tomorrow.
        But Then
I saw the facade
of hope falsely I see only
the fateful fingers calling me
As false shadows are cast upon
the wind as if it were a handful
of dirt crumbled into dust on an
Autumn breeze ruffling leaves dying.
But then my faith was being crumpled
into a dying breeze of autumn leaves fallen.

THE UNIVERSAL HAIR

I. Three baskets of darkness are splashed
against a starless night –
The moon's silhouette is leaking
thru restless clouds –
High in the Jemez mountains
the clouds have no boundaries,
yet their forms cling to the pines
in protozoaic postures –
Tonite, I slip away into the clouds
just as the swaying pines disappear
from me –
A strand of hair falls across my eyes
reminding me that I am a
universal hair and simultaneously smash
all dimensions of length, width, depth,
and time, time . . . time . . .

II. An era ago I was a pubic filament
drenched in sweat and blood on a
spear wounded chest, beneath a mouth
that mumbled in a dying and desperate
voice, "Forgive them Father, for they
know not what they do."
A mere hair becomes totally
immersed in every sensation of one who is dying.

III. In a microflash, I am a
trim, dark whisker on the chin of a
Greek teacher-philosopher in a city-state.
From a sunshine filled cell I witness
yet another senseless death of
dying for a principle instead of living for
a principle. A seemingly never ending

episode in the endless wasting of human life
as if it were something disposable. I fall dying.

IV. During the rhythm of respiration
I am transposed during the hesitation
of inhalation and exhalation.
        Time, having no dimensions nor
restriction carries me to the deck of a
Titanic ship Even tho' I'm an
eyelash, I can't see too good –
The fog and alcohol inhibit my view –
My scotch and water needs more ice –
I get more than I'll ever need –
A whole iceberg –
        Flailing and splashing in sub-zero
water, I sink and die.

V.   Just as an object thrown upwards hesitates
and then descends, it was during
the elapsed time of that particle of
hesitation that I found I was
transmigrated across several decades
not knowing a forwards, sideways,
nor reverse. I am transposed into
a thatch of hair arching an eye –
        In the back alley, a cold wind
trembles across a Parisian poet's hanged body.
Life began hanging from an umbilical cord
and now death hangs from an
imaginary queen's garter –
as the apron string stretched,
so did the corpse's neck – And I was
hanged and died.

VI.   A thought knows no time

and it is during that span
I transported myself to the courtyard
of a vietnamese politician –
I am a stubble of hair on the temple
of Bodhi Satva's body – The suicidal
monk sets himself aflame –
Now it's death by fire and there is
hope of escaping rebirth –

VII. Suddenly, I awaken –
I see the stars, not knowing which
one I'm on –
        The fog has lifted, the mountains
and the pines are real once again –
        Now I can see with a clear vision –
what has just happened,
letting it be a Light
to guide my life.

Fall 1970

RECENT IMPRINTS

FOR JULIA VINOGRAD

Last time I saw Beauty, she
was leaning over the craps table
shaking a pair of dice while I watched
her cleavage wiggle.

(It's funny how people who love & hate women
look at cleavage bending over, look
from the front above the neckline.
Yet, people who love & hate men
look at cleavage bending over, look
from the rear above the beltline.)

She, Beauty almost got away
clean as she cashed her chips,
tipped the doorman; they cuffed
her before a cabbie could screech his tires.
I heard the cops had her under
the investigation lights while she spilled her guts about Truth.
And the weeping never stops
No matter what the odds
or who the croupier is.

ANOTHER FOR JULIA VINOGRAD

I swore it was Truth leaning
in the doorway trying not to fall asleep
on his feet. After Beauty spilled
her guts to the cops, he was on the lam.
The word on the street was the Mob
put a Hit on him and the cops
wanted him as an accessory to a crime.
But this is America and the Truth can
hide anywhere; has been on the lam a long time.
Besides, who cares if you are Truth;
people ignore you for far less.
Just skip a few showers; step away from the razor;
fall out of favor with your landlord.
Jesus, Truth, show some class.
You used to hide out in a Beethoven piano sonata.
Whatever happened to your elegant taste for
math and science. You used to like confounding
everyone with contradictory facts about the smallest,
the hottest, and farthest away matter could be.
The way it used to matter to so many people;
Now, you just lie wheezing and geezing in the
doorway to the future.

* * *

W.C.C. quote:

Man alone is that creature
who cannot escape
suffering by flight.

* * *

I fell asleep, holding your hand
As a waning moon bathed my angst
in self-indulgent memories
of my dead brother Allen;
Washed clean by soft tears of love and loss.

MONOLOGUE FROM A DREAM

(for Joie Cook)
in a female voice

"No, that's not why Joie didn't show
up for her reading last Fri . . . .
You didn't know she got a job thru the dept.
of vocational rehabilitation.
A few evenings a week she
watches the ventilators. You
know, she sits and watches those
breathing machines attached
to all those comatose people at
S.F. General. Yes, the hospital's intensive
care floor. She sits there and if one
of the alarms rings she readjusts
the machine. You gotta be, smart tho'
It's helped her a lot you know,
with her self-respect; well now days
it's self esteem. She dresses nice and
not so much make-up, you know, balanced
She even wears beautiful ear rings —
the gold kind that shine and dangle.
She's got a new boyfriend. The Pope.
Now, I'm not much for June/December affairs
but they look good together him
with those flowing robes and her
with her nice new skirts and blouses.
They talk a lot you know. She's
been trying to talk to him about
Virgin Births because
they can't do it the other way
him being married to God and all . . .

NOT AWAKE BUT

On my way to work in the morning
Gotta get to work – Got only 5-7 minutes
Gotta get out the door, get
driving, going, doing – Only 5-7 minutes
but before I'm out the door the
radio announcer announces Beethoven's Birthday
And starts playing the Moonlight sonata
And the moon shines into me from the hands on the piano on the
compact disc on the player
in the radio station studio and air carries the
invisible silence into the room and the radio's
sounds pour into my ears while I lean
against the cold morning kitchen wall
dripping with tea kettle's moisture hearing Beethoven
again and this time it's tears welling in my eyes and
breathing is deep and syncopated
my knees are flexing and I am in flux feeling the
sensual radiance across two centuries
of pen and ink and pain.

LIBRARY CODE VIOLATION

crouching, hiding
surreptitiously sliding
half day old sandwich of cheese
beneath the table of books
not wanting librarians to see
me eating, spilling, dropping crumbs
not wanting others to assume
i draw cockroaches
with my actions

the old neighborhoods

i like the old neighborhoods best
where it takes at least six people
to change a tire – two matriarchs
to supervise and advise the married
and console the unwedded
two patriarchs to prattle about
how it was in the good old days
and how it could've been if they'd
of been the boss back then
and one big, strapping macho
buck to break the rust on the lug nuts
and a youngster, eager and almost able
to do the rest of the work and sweat
but what i like best is the loud music
it's always tops with me.

WELTERING

too old too soon
too wise too late

enlightenment allowed me too see
the enormity of my stupidity

today, all i know is what i don't know

it's been a tough day being enlightened

so i took the clerk's advice; had a nice day

then i took off
the rest of my life

BIG TONY

(for JoAnna)

Some tried to sell me that it was poetry,
others poetic justice to explain another of
nature's injustices.
It was frost said a few knowingly
where the warmth coursing thru the body
collided against the cold of the environment,
condensing frost and freezing, crystallizing
time and fracturing sunlight into sparkles.

It was uremic frost. Crystals of urine
that escaped from the blood stream
oozed their way thru the skin swallowing
its own debris. Waste and piss
surfaced to escape itself.
Urine settled on the skin and reeked.

Thanks to chemistry times speed divided by modern
we have better ways of dying hideously
when kidneys and liver fail

But beyond yourself Big Tony
on a wall in a shop in a city
along Route 66,
there hangs framed a
kachina carved and painted
by your hands, eyes, and heart
Framed, hanging, suspended
in Beauty for far longer than your human body.

TIME MELT

Going to Susanne's where
Susanne and husband feed me
chicken stock, eggs, and rice soup.
They tell me how the flu
has bugged their children.
Slurping is a new found pleasure.
Their children recovered
and run the restaurant in the future
while my soup cools enough to slurp
and I can't remember the time
tunnel we just went through
of soup stock and chicken.

SUSANNE'S

It's Susanne's soup again
But this time I'm not sick.
Don't have a cold or the flu.
A little more alone, separateness, less afraid.
The sunsets are the same colors and
the moon still waxes to fullness.
Tides pull and push, pine needles fall from branches
of evergreens. The fog appears
in valleys, along the rivers, by the bays,
near the oceans, and along the coastal hills.
But it's o.k. because I can cross the midlines.
I can hear Doppler's effect on passing trains
in the early morning darkness.
And I can breathe; I can swim.
I can dance and can hike and fly my kite,
I can name flowers in a garden,
I feel your pain and joy and anger,
I am pulsing with passionate openness
from living, tempering this with
compassionate letting go. There is
more falling away as the
glaciers move.
There is falling away as a glacier moves
southerly out to sea in sheer terror and beauty.
Splashing into blue liquid is a huge cascade
of melting ice and taking in heat.

FOR HENRY REED

Today's Lesson:
learning to concentrate
amongst the noises
it is quiet inside
i can hear great
vacuums of empty
space chanting bliss
amongst themselves

Again Asian cafe
grousing about past
how it was, i told ya so
how it should've been
and could have been
still the slurping – Noddles
rice, fish, fowl – Across
deep lines of facial time
eating and sweating
while grease smells
in the air of frying, roasting
and cooking – Money changing
hands while the talking rattles
and prattles – Black hair
some with grey – Eyes brown
some with grey senile arcs
while white noise fills
my ears – i am emptying
of my own noises and
i hear voices speak
to me,
    bodisattva
    is within
    (Pay or Wash)
  ". . . the bill, sir . . ."

DECEMBER

It's Winter and it's another Asian cafe.
I am waiting for another piled high plate of fried rice,
vegetables and sea forms wok fried fast and hot.
The teapot will steam moistly out the spout
but I am surprised.
"Hot soup, free today, I give you, it's cold Winter, warm you . . .
You need it today . . . No christmas for you . ."
She knows. She smiles.
The outer skin is reptilian, rough, sandpaper texture,
Broken by her smile and nurturing motherly eyes,
Warming this loneliness into corn starch, water,
soy bean curd, scallions and chicken muscle swimming
in the simmering broth.
I am grateful in my writing.
I am grateful my mother is still alive
despite our geographic differences.
Some Jews choose to be lightning their lights,
spinning their dreidels and savoring their chocolates.
There are sweets for Christians; pastries and frankincense.
Pagans chase the darkness with their drunken hedonism
of Saturnalia overeating.
In December, it is warm inside despite
the northern hemisphere's outside coldness.

* * *

Loopholes:
information
education
knowledge
wisdom

SUSANNE'S SOUP

It's the warmth from Susanne's Soup
that keeps me coming back for more;
strength and warmth in the tea
turning tepid in my hands.
The lights have yellowed over with the cooking of oils
and meat grease. The people whose lungs
exhaled tobacco smoke have hazed the windows
and walls. Susanne's young teenage
daughters painted the interior during Winter's
school holdays.
Now everyone calls ahead and orders
carry outs, to go, llevar.
This emotional popsicle generation wants
culture to go. An aestheticism they can carry,
eat while running, driving back to their lairs,
burrow in and feed their young.
Eat it, predigest it and then regurgitate
it for their offspring. A whole generation
may never see/smell/hear the sizzle of rice
and meat grease
who will never know the heartache
of being alive, not knowing the heartache
of living.
Not knowing the dreams smashed
by reality, by money, rent and credit.
Not knowing that a dream can survive.
Survive so long that the succor of success outweighs
all the heartaches of crying desk clerks.
Missing the fire from the light that forges iron ore
into fine tempered steel.

I gave her my coat of freedom.
She tried it on; liked it.
Made one of her own almost like mine
And gave my coat of freedom
back five years later.

* * *

Oh, Laura

She feels the pain in her beak

as this bird from paradise pecks

at the shell from the inside to break

into the next universe.

* * *

O, Melinda

I'd rather be

a little crazy

and love you a lot

than not.

* * *

O'Mary

She had the courage

to pattern her life

after a woman –

herself

VINCENT'S SPRING, 1889

You are already oscillating within
You're multitudes of vortices
Patterns of chaos are vibrating
and swirling around you and within
your creativity.

Vincent, artists are always going to differ
And it's going to be years before anyone
has the courage to feel the way you do

Your threatening Paul with a knife
didn't help to make your point.
The depression of your guilt
and the same is turned
inward on yourself; and now
you've mutilated your ear so you
won't hear the screech so
you can just see the colors and paint

you know there's not much time left
(A year and a half tops) 29 July 1890

You're back in the hospital again
to recuperate, so you can paint the hospital
but still you still have the cypresses to do
and you're not finished with your yellows.
You've got to do the fields, the crows
(yes you know) the stars at night
beside the gas light, shivering stars
and steeples of faith shaking in the darkness
(yes you know)

"This exhibition is assembled for those few
who still believe that what is immediately
grasped is not necessarily the best." 1892 March
An artist named R.N. Doland Holst in an introduction.

FINDING MY FEET

week #8 Feeling for My Soles

Not the Western emotional landmined, psychological
boobytrapped,
intellectual pitfall soul of Plato the dead
but the soles of my feet on the land.
Just as the sole fish is feeling the
bottom of the water feeding in the
dark, cold currents of water world.

Rocking back and forth,
lift big toe then shifting
to lift heel as the spine
dangles from a silk thread.

The pelvic girdle swaying
hip bones in the ball sockets
stretching ligamentously towards
letting go to allow filling
up with creativity and clarity.

Returning home, I'm on the porch
rocking as the autumnal equinox,
full moon rises, shining through
cleared sky of evening coolness.
I inhale the power too deeply,
begin to cry; crying and grieving
over past deaths in this life time.
Sister, father, brother, grandparents,
cousin, and within this lifetime, another lover.

Changing, growing there is great pain in this learning.
There is pain with letting go. The memories are stored
in the endorphinogenic areas of the ligaments,
tendons, soft tissues along the meridians.
The initiate is bent over,
doubled over with crying
and too much human feeling and not enough
self compassion and too much letting go.
There must be more falling away from the clinging,
the past, someone else's scripts, someone else's role
of a dead person; died months ago
in the piedmont and flatlands of
San Francisco's East Bay.
There can be no redemption, salvation
or resurrection, only the present
moment of the molted one who
phoenixed into the here and now
as a reincarnated poet, philosopher,
teacher, nurse and Michael.

* * *

from innocence to naivete

(for Mariah & Anne)

you're older now you're six
you tell your mother
how silly you were
when you were three
how you thought the moon
was a bunch of angels
and know you know better
your six and it's just the moon.

"and i . . . told the stars
my questions"
All My Pretty Ones:
"Young" A. Sexton

The train rumbles on the tracks
for once in this life time, I'm unamused
at the existing nihilism and negativity
of drunks and angry warriors. I'm
feeling a dance in the soles of my feet
hearing a melody line clear in my muscles
seeing sunlight bounce is now enough
to make me happy as a smile stretches
across my mouth as the muscles relax in my face
the smell of women on me, a new lover, who's like
the dance of sambas across hard wood floors
working against the bar, spontaneity and instrumentation
streaming consciously down the saxophones neck
into another time/space continuum because
all because
she said, " I hope you enjoy your fantasies . . ."
I did and fell asleep while Vladamir Askenazy
fingered "Hammerklavier," the piano sonata
filling up the reality of sleepy night time
of emptiness.

Reawakening, I smiled, thought I was
on a train's syncopated rocking seat
of dozing sleep, smiled, realized
it was her voice laughing,
her eyes smiling.
Getting on my feet, I returned to my bed
and waited for the alarm clock's harshness
in dreamless sleep.

I SEE THE STARS. I HEAR THE ROLLING THUNDER.

I remember greatness in a poem,
In a painting, in a musical piece,
and when it first came to me.
It wasn't from some high school teacher
or college professor. It came from me, from within me.

And seeing sculpture and statuary
with Beauty twirling a noose
invited me to try; somewhere
within the strength to resist
the petty charm of prostitution and pimping
hecklers. It all came from within me and
without someone else to separate shaft from shit
and con from crap. But it was always me
and from within me. Not like some pre-tried
authority-critic, expert or scholar
but me. And danced within myself feeling
like a grown-up; I was adult and now no one
can tell me my own beauty but me.
No, it wasn't as if Beauty was unfair or unequal
more like a stone, a nugget
when I gave in I caved in inward within me.
Seduction can take you out in more
ways than one can ever expect
no matter how smart, crafty, clever or wise.

The scary feelings of being sober & sane
the tightrope no net no balance pole
but worst of all no audience to applaud
the darkness of blackness and abysmal
nightfall of cold emptiness
at least when trapeze flyers fall
the crowds gasp; the net the ground
catches you
but sober & sane falling means
hitting bottom and rearranging pieces

Now in a faint flash realizing
just how sick how frightened
by bottled reality uncorked, unscrewed
I was I choose sane & sober
I choose trusting myself.

* * *

The wheel still spins
we're all on the manadella
the beast is the phoenix
there's always too much dust
death and ashes that
cry for the phoenix and cycles
cycles that expand themselves
enough to include us.

* * *

I got no idea 'a love . . .

Fast Eddie; The Hustler

passion disguised as intellectualism

FROM INSIDE THE PATHOLOGY

(a line from Bruce Isaacson)

The call, my sister, you'd better sit for this one
death raised its head from reptilian lagoon
devouring mammals   Bloody, gory
Avenging the Ice Age and Crashing Meteors.
From Texas, from Illinois, from St. Thomas
the Virgin Islands to New Mexico
the body will be flown
it'll take several days
that's good I'm the nurse
for a three day summer camp
I promised the citizens, the clients
my patients, the mentally challenged
association for retarded citizens
in a frustrating confrontation of control
I teeter on a cataclysmic abyss of abusiveness
request, refusal (on guard) raised voices
shouting (check) shoving (stalemate or checkmate)
slapping avoided, aggression avoided, averted (detente)
regroup, loss of control, mandella spinning
my life spiralling   free fall   my brother's
open casket yawns (deja vu)   the mountains
summer camp, lost youth, scalding tears
of adulthood, the anger is real   in place (on guard)
spinning, spiralling, free fall
out of control emotions, anger of frustration
fences unclimbed – unvined walls tall
from within my own darkness comes the anger
Anger

FOR KAY BOYLE (AND EMILY LEIDER)

Drowning in their own shallowness, they pine
away and piss away their youthful ardor
on romantic notions about skies full of clouds
and stars.

Instead of saving themselves, fattening their
wallets or attaining their own enlightenment,
they want to save a world that despises
them, would keep them out of Eutopia or anyone's
Republic.

They deserve, we all deserve, to die spitting blood
and shitting on ourselves for the stupidity
of not knowing, for not realizing only music
can change the world – only pure music.

ARIZONA, COLORADO, NEW MEXICO, & UTAH

        meteoric ride thru tunnels
at 70 mph as lites blur . . .
        the fossil fuel burners choke
out smoke in Four Corners, USA
        electricity crackles 1,000 miles away by
wires to the San Francisco Bay
for BART ride under the Bay

DISTANT APPARITION

I. I guess that day we went fishing together
we knew each other the best.
With no siblings to rival,
we were both old enough
to understand the unspoken,
the unsaid, the quiet, the solitude.
You even let me catch more
Sunfish than you and now
I understand your fatigue;
it was circulatory, vascular —
the heart was tired.

II. When you died I felt guilty
as if I should have loved
you more
more openly
more intensely
more publicly
more often
I felt the moorings cut
away from the quay as I
drifted into ancient celtic fog
banked with insecurity, intuiting;
drifting with the Gaelic currents
and the tides of the Book of Kells
of uncertainty and antiquity
leaving me vastly alone
in endlessness
awaiting disappointment.

III. Perhaps I inherited your guilt
the guilt that you felt
in your job's stability and
thirty-five years of security.
It was guilt you inherited
from your father, along with your disappointment
when he was unable to find a job
better than a farmer, elevator operator,
bellhop, custodian, complicated by drinking
and his guilt of being Catholic
and his father being Irish
from the old country, a dirt farmer.

IV. But father, your quiet stoicism
has dissolved itself upon
the DNA rubble heap of a generation
that survived prosperity, depression,
war, and prosperity.
My father, dear dad, the authority
figure, disciplinarian, barely
aged with dignified, greying of accepting
the next generation into adulthood.
You died, yes you did; it was awhile
back but now i recall it all.
Your distant apparition conjures itself
and returns the way rainstorms
and memories do.

EXACTLY THE WAY FRUIT TREES BLOSSOM BEFORE THE LAST SNOWFALL

Love is a straight jacket and then you're tied
by a rope around your ankles and hanged
up side down dangling till someone you don't
even know sets the rope on fire and you have ten
minutes to get out of this straight jacket called
love.

It's a bachelor party, the wedding party
St. Valentine's Day, your birthday —
have another drink, smoke, snort, something
to eat, fatten you up, limber up your muscles.
Escape by divorce, suicide, insanity
work-oholism have already been tried.
Escape has not, it's repeated,
not been written, spoken, learned
known or agreed upon but the straight jacket
feels good, you bought it, she/he/they made it
for you, just for you. You've been fitted
snap, click the buckles, the straps are locked.
You feel she/he/they hug you with lies
and illusions. You're beginning to hug
yourself at the waist
as the ropes are being tied to your ankles.
Self deceit and delusion hoist you up as you dangle.
There is the smell of burning rope
as the clock ticks starkly in your ears towards ten.
When the fire burns thru you fall and keep
falling till you hit the center of the earth
where your essence is immediately returned
to trillions of hydrogen atoms and the entropy
from which you came reshuffles you home.

ABOUT NURSING

It's the secrets people tell me
that I like the best.
All the dirty laundry that needs airing
about the substances and people
they abused.
Love turned to hate; control dominance
ruthless business ventures
pouring their hearts
spilling their guts
about how they
cheated at what, on whom,
and why.
The things they wanted, lusted after
got and lost . . . the people, the relatives
friends fucked over just to get
something, somewhere, somebody
tainted and tawdry, every day
is Yom Kippur . . . every evening
Good Friday Confessional
the nights are even more insane
irrational and unbelievable
The Bad thing is I can't really
tell you mine
By the way what's yours
I'm not in it for the money
I'm in it for the secrets.

Nurses eat their young. Marilyn Shalley-Damberg 1992.
Perfectionist cannabalize their mistakes.

Nurses eat their young.
Perfectionists cannabalixe their mistakes
Perfectionists cannabalize their mistakes.
Perfectionists cannabalize their mistakes.
Being a tough bird from the philosophy school,
I was frequently eaten by yet another mother figure
and then regurgitated by yet another nurse authority figuree
and then regurgitated by yet another nurse authority figure. :
It's happening now and only in my angst can I feel it.
Like some grade-B Kafkaesque scenario yet to be written
I am metamorphosing into a real nurse hatchling.
The exoskeleton is a precarious fit like a bulky suit
of medieval armor, I RATTLE ALONG on my swayback stead.

REVISION OF A TRANSLATION FROM SANSKRIT
(in two voices)

Oh, holy mendicant monk

I see you eat meat.

Oh, yes, it's fine when you dine
and goes so well with red wine
but i most prefer the whites.

The taste of the grape on the lips

of the aesthetic one . . .

Yes, by all means the women
of the night loosen
with a glass or two of white wine.

Loose women; who pays the expense

for such extravagances . . .

Oh, the horses pay well
and i boost a fancy car
to a chop shop for chump change.

Gambling, thievery from the

enlightened holiness . . .

Well, yes, i took the vow
of poverty, you know.

The blues are back on my back
off the rack in the sack
the big boys want to play
long ball, hard ball
wanting some dying
to entertain them
keep them entertained
keep the bottom line
from bottoming up
the only scene that saves me
from myself was this lady
dying and telling me
the only things worth
recalling are the pastures
with horses and greenness
fog rolling back in the
morning to let in the
sunshine
the leaves swaying
their branches
tumbled by the winds
emeralds in the creeks
fussing over rocks
the sounds of the oceans
can't you hear the call
the seeing of sky blueness
children splashing
swimming in the buff
crystal clarity
fracturing sunlite
and color giving up its
secret hues

THE FIRST NOBLE TRUTH

feelings of cold smoothness, of round metal everywhere
everywhere in the darkness; the smell of nitrates
and petrochemicals; hearing hydrolix
opening to light and coldness with very little
heat; even a little heat is better than crystallization
the opening is oblong white rectangle
some blue then brown but back to whiteness
electronix engage, hydrolix again, the mechanical
levers lift and there is release; there is rolling
followed by falling, falling away
coldness of air but more heat
falling into white and moisture colder than rain
falling faster till falling fades
then a countryside, a city, a street
people staring upward with eyes open
everyone is exploding all around
hair and skin reach flash point first then flesh
having taken life and NOW Becoming
I AM BOMB

u.s. planes flew more than 100,000 sorties
each plane dropped more than 3 bombs
more than half of the bombs exploded
carpet bombing, saturation bombing
Feb '91

Re: The oil wars
Misery is always rich and expensive.

Anonymous Quote from the Prattle of the Crowd

"I had a dream last nite
and as clear to me now
as it were yesterday . . ."

THE THIRD NOBLE TRUTH

> "There is nothing like sin for
> the removal of complacency . . .
> John Steinbeck, 1951.

The fire in the fireplace burned
evenly and warm while the cat
stretched herself and relaxed
in the luxuriant heat of the fire.
The kid, six, played upstairs with her
playthings and hummed a tune
of innocence and nonsense.
You had gone out to the grocery
store or something for something.
And it was quiet while I read my book
about Steinbeck and his book.
And thru the quiet of Sunday evening
solitude, I heard the 7:45
whistle its way across the railroad
crossings and I tried to resist
but temptations weaken even those
stronger than me and I'm almost gone
till a log sparks and pop brings me back.
Older and easier to stay than go
but tomorrow, again, the train's whistle will blow.

ON CRITICIZING WOMEN'S POETRY

that I should be a leashed swine
rooting for truffle

I am the Aging Antelope
Zig Zag and Zoom
betrayed by Zest and Zeal

The Zebra herd has headed
out across the Veldt
Predatory crouching
motions disturb the grasses
Leaping & Bolting
The hunger of the jaguar blurs
in the bush
The running, the chase
continues, has begun
as it has thru the eons
of predator et prey
Adrenaline, epinephrine
and endorphins
gush as nerves fire
and muscles contract
Reflexing, rapidly
Neurons arcing
My stride has been broken
Paw's claws break skin to bleed and blister
The center of balance & gravity spins
wobbles while footing falters
All I know is now
Now all I know is breathing
feeling hot, wet breath of deep breathing
feline – Saliva on my fur
Escaping the first bite; coup
I have been touched by the Jaguar's
mouth and teeth are beyond my ears
Pawing jaguar spinning antelope
the weight weighs badly off center
timing is terribly confused; muscles contract

out of sync., nerve fibers fire aflutter fibrillating.
Two front paws over front haunches of antelope
It's all this head bobbing across the horizon line
the feet feel funny, front in back, right is left
the jaguar's teeth and mouth are beyond my ears
Two front paws over my front haunches
press down and smother prey with shear
weight and strength. There is slack, relax,
limpness and falling away from pain.
Jaguar leans down in prominence and dominance
feline fangs puncture neck trachea and arteries
bites the throat, the breath & breathing change.
My throat, the trachea collapse, carotid neck
vessels punctured there is bleeding
there is no more breathing – gasping and
struggle worsens the bleeding and tearing
by feline's canine teeth . . . eye-teeth with eyes
fangs tear bigger holes, the holes torn bigger
the air is going everywhere but into the air
outside everywhere with the air

Aged Antelope, interloper limp hangs
in the grasp in the jaws of
the jaguar, of feline huntress jaguar
Antelope dangles from mouth of speedy, spotted cat
Hunted and hanging lifeless, dragged listlessly
back to be fed to yapping cubs
No lotus blooms; the water
is so still stagnant; wealth
and corpulence is killing
the lilies.
Hyenas and Vultures
get ideas and hungry.

SALLY'S DANCE

That's the way I remember my lusting youth as innocence,
naivete, stupidity and ignorance. Shattering subatomic
particles was after midnight in the blue, white, light of
cigarette smoke filling the singles bar, overfilled with
people and overamped and undercooked music. After midnight and
the booze was sloushing around while vendors and buyers jostled
in the meat market for a position to see and/or be seen.
Just as I was about to ask about your dusky, cachexic, toxic
skin's complexion that had rusted with the hard years of too
much, too many hard powders, a jostler crashed my icy drink
down my front side. It was like a prophesy, an omen. I felt a
wave of unworthy shame drench me as the lost and unreclaimable
innocence of ignorance and youth diffused into the air with
the other smoke exhaled by dragon's breath.
The giggling girls of late adolescence and early teenage
boys with lust filled fantasies crashing pajama parties
are scared window peepers stumbling into the bushes of
sexual awakenings.
Faster than cigarettes burn or spilled liquor can dry, I
realized some girls grow up to be women junkies, strung out
and desperate for intimacy and affection with human beings
instead of the powders they dance to late at night.
But you soak up the light and it's dark all around you.
Leaving the bar, I am not the same person who entered.
The worm of reality turns in the apple and romantic notions
of history are turned for full view intertwining life/death
with youth/age. The seams are showing on the seamier side of reality.
It's a bitter taste this awareness, this realizing, this knowing and
I know why tonite I needed a drink. Sometimes the numbness
makes the reality slow down enough to regain something not lost.
But the numbness doesn't help. The rage of the horror and tragic
truth shows itself like the emptiness
of Black Holes on an astronomer's
photograph of the cosmos.

FEELING THE DARKNESS

(for Carla because she knew my secrets)

Two women, too afraid to be in love.
Fucking with their dysfunctional men
who sleep away; sleeping, facing their walls.

Fucking with their dysfunctional men
would have to do for now
while they talked and fires burned.

Forging their new friendships
their perfect love of themselves
each other and each other's pain.

They feel beyond themselves
and in front of the fireplace
they feel the warmth of the fire.

Together in their separate separatedness
they feel the warmth on the skin of their faces.

On the skin of their necks
they feel the cool of the nite on their skins.

The truth and beauty of being human, women, alone
and of loving despite each other's dysfunctionalisms.

COMFORT

We have no men to comfort us
this night. Two sisters who
stare into the fire, our eyes are
those of leopards. My lover far
from me, and her man sleeps,
his face turned toward the wall.
There is silence here, the
crackling of the flames is small,
unjustified. We do not speak,
there are no words we have not
spoken, her sorrow poured into
my ears, my fears into hers, We
are alone together, too lonely
to look up at stars or think of
tomorrow. We are far beyond
even comforting one another.

from *A Year Of Joy and Sorrow*
poems by Carla Kandinsky

FEELING THE LIGHT

(for Melinda because she knows my secrets)

Two persons, no longer too afraid to be in love
Not necessarily with each other
but with the courage to always share
To be honest, to be free, to be open to the
cosmic universe of existence

Laughing with the child inside
Swimming, running, flying a kite
diving or snorkeling together
but always separate and alone
as they were born

Living they feel beyond themselves
and each other and each others' pain

fires burning and everyone's growing
towards the sun the yellow light
of saffron of white truth
and blinding beauty

LARRY BLAKE'S

focus on a flake of
        sawdust on the floor
find the center of
        the universe while
the rest of you
twists, shimmies and shakes
with rhythm to
patter pattern of
the drummer

It's new, the old silence is back
but this time it's improved; it's approved
we agree; agreeing that to rest is a need
we must meet. The daily assault is overwhelmingly cacophony.
This silence is not preceded by and accompanied by
death knells and cancerous spreading.

This silence is agreed upon mutually
        is listening to ourselves
        is a rest stop
        is punctuated with laughter and giggling
These silences are punctuated with laughter and giggling
These silences are rest stops

These silences have ears that see the sound waves
before they bounce and echo against the rigid
landing into the past

These silences beg for merciful forgiveness
        from the din of reality
                beg for an escape into the light
        warmth and motion of comfort

These silences have soft hair and eyes
with deep black pupils
have terse firm lips curving
shining in the sunlight's shimmer
have cheekbones and magazine models'
waistlines but the skin is creased and oozes living
and chancing for a glimpse of luck
acceptance or approval
have moles, birthmarks and imperfections

These silences arrogantly presuppose everyone
understands them; smiling with precious stones
and metal in their ear lobes

can't be seen because of other silences
standing in front of other silences reaching
and holding on to commuter straps

These silences dance in bubbles of protected serenity
are polymorphic
changing dynamically before I can kiss
them with my ear's tympany

These silences
know of ginger
taste of rose
smell of thyme
feel of sage
are rubbed of alum
blinded by jasmine

These silences have ears that see the sound waves
before they bounce and echo against the rigid
landing in the past and I can't hold
the silence back anymore and shout
Prattling romantically; digressing.

DOUBLETRUTH

Grass grows greener
when it's raining.

OTHER POSSIBILITIES

for Chitra Divakaruni

One is free from depression
when self-esteem is based
on authenticity of one's
own feelings . . .
Alice Miller, 1971
The Drama of the Gifted Child

The monk, he smells aromas; cooking seafood
or meat, some chicken, poultry, duck maybe.
He jumps the monastery walls becoming
a beggar who is hungry only to meet his
fellow fallow monks begging for casserole.
His fear of being caught is lessened by his hunger
for forbidden meats.

Scheming father buys meats and fishes
because his wife no longer needs another grown
daughter. Her fears greater than being caught.
The parents have no shame only a plan.
And now the shame of an unwed daughter
is greater than the fears of entrapment of monks
or enslavement of daughters. The Chang family
needs to continue.

Here in a Chinatown restaurant, we select
from the menu, Monk Jumping Casserole.
The uneasiness of being discovered lingers aromatically.
like the greasy steam from the Sizzling dishes.
Anticipation of discovery outweighs our fears.
The shame and guilt of having lived too hard
for so long is no longer delicious just prolonged torment
without enough rest.

Thriving towards sunlight; unexplored feelings explode
into accepting growth and where our contradictions intersect.
We mirror each other's vulnerability with respectful empathy.
And you say, "Yes." to my proposal; echoing intangibles.
The smell of the imagined is very different
from the taste on the tongue; this I have lessoned
after too many years of reality without purity.

Three postscript quotes from Alice Miller:
. . . because the truth often would be unbearable . . .
. . . for many people the truth is so essential
that they must pay dearly for its loss . . .
. . . the truth always causes much pain before
giving us a new sphere of freedom . . .

CUT FLOWERS

The flowers I bought today are in reality
in a bunch and half dead, petals
falling away and letting go leaves

For me they are beautiful, the most
gorgeous ever. I bought them
for myself; I'm greedy I had
to have them – They have color
and fragrance that I don't have
in my solo self, half living
I can taste and feel them
behind my eyes and wrap
my feelings around them
in sensual eroticism
the flowers want to feel me, also
I want these feelings to fill me
they're honest feelings tho' incomplete
I want these feelings more than
I want the loneliness, emptiness
and aching
I feel the flowers and smell them
just long enough to get from here
at the table, at the paper, at the pen
and into bed smelling and feeling
till I can get to sleep and forgetfulness
I am dancing with flowers
yellow daisies and chrysanthemums sing in the nite.

LATE ROMANTICISM

At night, I lie on the bed in the dark and wait
for stars to come from behind clouds,
for the waning moon to rise.
And I realize what a mess I've made of my life
and how self-indulgent and self-absorbed I've become.
        In darkness, I eat a sandwich while
the radio plays something classical, Poulenc maybe.
But I fall asleep before the moon rises
or the clouds can lift enough to allow
the stars' shine to penetrate the eternal blue
in the blackness of dark.

MUCHOS SOMOS SERIES

Number 1	*Gurgle of Little Feet,* Tom Ross*
Number 2	*Behind Dark Glasses,* Karen Lee Hones*
Number 3	*Chronicle,* Edward Mycue*
Number 4	*I See America Daily,* Harold Norse*
Number 5	*Bronka Stooler Boo Boo Boo,* Pablo Cuneo
Number 6	*Wheatberry Fantasies,* Garrett Lambrev*
Number 7	*Musical Trees,* H.D. Moe*
Number 8	*Voices and People Forgotten,* Louis Cuneo*
Number 9	*Jazz Pajamas,* H. D. Moe*
Number 10	*Lights/Letters – Words For Adelle,* Jack Foley
Number 11	*Going to China and Other Places,* Mary Rudge
Number 12	*Decade: The 1990's,* John Curl
Number 13	*Passing Moments,* Louis Cuneo
Number 14	*Old Man Klute'n the Pear Tree,* Edwin Massey, Jr.
Number 15	*The Troubles,* Dale Jensen
Number 16	*Fifty Cantos From the Land of Nod,* Edwin Massey, Jr.
Number 17	*Light Blooms,* Michael Thomas Kelly

*Out of print